AF211880

C.T. MITCHELL

TRAVEL SECRETS

The Ultimate Guide to Travelling the Unconventional Way, Learn About Interesting Travel Destinations For a More Fun and Rewarding Vacation

Descrierea CIP a Bibliotecii Naţionale a României
C.T. MITCHELL
   TRAVEL SECRETS. The Ultimate Guide to Travelling the Unconventional Way, Learn About Interesting Travel Destinations For a More Fun and Rewarding Vacation / C.T. Mitchell – Bucharest: Editura My Ebook, 2020
   ISBN

C.T. MITCHELL

TRAVEL SECRETS

The Ultimate Guide to Travelling the Unconventional Way, Learn About Interesting Travel Destinations For a More Fun and Rewarding Vacation

My Ebook Publishing House
Bucharest, 2020

CONTENTS

CHAPTER 1

TOP FAITH-BASED TRAVEL LOCATIONS

A pilgrimage to a religious site is a once in a lifetime dream for many travelers. The Holy Land, home of the roots to Islam, Judaism and Christianity, is a destination many travelers aspire to visit at least once in their lives. Here are some of the top faith-based travel destinations in the Holy Land.

Jerusalem is a top tourist attraction for visitors of many faiths. The golden-topped Dome of the Rock is sacred to both Jews and Muslims as the site of the first and second Jewish temples – the original was said to have been built by King Solomon and held the Ark of the Covenant. The Dome of the Rock is now an Islamic shrine at Temple Mount where Muslims believe that the prophet Muhammad ascended to heaven accompanied by the angel Jibril or Gabriel. The Dome of the Rock also covers the Foundation Stone, said to be the holiest site for Jews. The Al Aqsa Mosque, also part of the Temple

Mount, is the third most important Islamic mosque, after Mecca and Medina.

Adjacent to the Dome of the Rock is the Western Wall or Wailing Wall. The wall survives as part of the second temple and part of the original Temple Mount. For centuries, this has been a major religious location for Jews due to its proximity to the Holiest of Holies in the temple itself. Traditionally, visitors write a prayer and place it in the wall.

The Church of the Holy Sepulcher in Jerusalem is an important destination for Christians, who have been making pilgrimages to the site since the 4th century. Located in the old Christian quarter of Jerusalem, this church covers the location where Jesus was said to have been crucified, buried and resurrected.

The Via Dolorosa is the pathway that Jesus is reported to have taken after he was sentenced by Pontius Pilate and is known as the most sacred Christian paths in the world.

Mount Zion, also in Jerusalem, marks the location of both the Last Supper and the tomb of King David, making this an important site for both Christian and Jewish visitors.

In Egypt, Mt. Sinai is a popular destination where many believe Moses was given the Ten Commandments. Others interested in following in the footsteps of Moses might consider visiting Mt. Nebo in Jordan, where it is believed that Moses first viewed the Promised Land and was later buried.

Every Muslim is encouraged to visit Mecca one in their lives. Located in the Makkah province in Saudi Arabia, Mecca is Islam's spiritual center because it is considered the birthplace of the prophet Mohammed and the place where the Quran was revealed to him. The journey to Mecca is known as the Hajj, a trip that all Muslims who have the means should take at least once in their lifetime. The visit is supposed to give the traveler forgiveness for all their sins. Non-Muslims are prohibited from entering Mecca. In Mecca, one can see the Mesjid al-Haram, the largest mosque in the world. The Zam Zam well, reputed to contain the purest water on heaven and earth. You can also see Hira, in Jibal al-noor, The Mountain of Light, a cave in which Abraham received his first verses of the Quran from the angel Jibril, also known as Gabriel.

Wherever you go, bring comfortable shoes, dress for the weather and bring a sense of adventure. You'll be traveling in the footsteps of millions of religious faithful and seeing not only major sacred sites, but also beautiful wonders of the world.

CHAPTER 2

EXOTIC UNDER THE SEA EXPLORATIONS

Love the idea of exploring the depths of the sea? There are all kinds of exotic under the sea trips available, from snorkeling and scuba diving to underwater hotels. Here are some suggestions for your next trip.

For many people, scuba diving is the first trip that comes to mind when considering under the sea explorations. There are all kinds of scuba diving trips that can fit into any budget. Whether it's the Caribbean, Mexico's Mayan Riviera, the Florida Keys, or even New England, many of these exotic locations offer scuba instruction as well as a front row seat to coral reefs, exotic fish and shipwrecks.

Swim encounters are popular in many parts of the world. The opportunity to swim with dolphins is a vacation experience offered throughout Mexico and the Caribbean. There are also swim with shark experiences – these extreme diving tours can include snorkeling lessons or scuba instruction while others require that you swim with a certified dive guide. Underwater whale watching and opportunities to swim with humpback whales opportunities are also growing in popularity. Because of concern for aggressive behavior, snorkeling tourists can observe whale behavior by letting the whale approach them, rather than the other way around. Swimmers hear their whale songs, and have an unforgettable, exhilarating experience. Other companies allow tourists to view wales from underwater pods.

If exploring underwater ruins is more your cup of tea, consider The Museum of Underwater Modern art below sea level in Cancun, Mexico. Jason de Caires Taylor built the more than 400 statues, made from environmentally friendly clay. Hauntingly beautiful his underwater statues depict regular people doing ordinary things such as sitting at a desk, reading the newspaper or standing in crowds – the underwater aspect and fish swimming through them adds an eerie quality. Visitors take a speedboat ride to the site and then a snorkeling tour through the museum.

If a dive is never enough time underwater, you might consider booking an underwater hotel. Jules' Undersea Lodge, located in Key Largo, Florida, is one scuba attraction that offers not only an undersea park but also a hotel. Hotel patrons can see a variety of marine life, from barracuda to the occasional manatee as well as participate in lab programs. Other resort/spa hotels in the works include the proposed Poseidon Undersea Resort Park in Fiji. Tourists can enjoy all the comforts of a spectacular luxury hotel while viewing marine life in their natural habitat.

Some of the proposed offerings include rooms with Jacuzzis from which guest can experience panoramic views of underwater marine life, lighted feeding areas for feeding marine life, and instruction in piloting three person submersible vehicles. There is a private jet available to fly guests from Nadi International Airport to the main island, Viti Levu. There is a bar, restaurant and even an underwater wedding chapel. Although reservations are not yet Being taken, interested parties can sign up to be notified when the time comes. The resort also does not yet list a price for its accommodations, but ensure visitors that the price for this five star luxury resort with will be worth every penny.

Whether you're interested in snorkeling, scuba diving, swimming with the fishes or riding in a submersible, there's something for everyone in a vacation under the sea.

CHAPTER 3

RAINFORESTS, TROPICS
AND WATERFALL VACATIONS

Looking for an exciting tropical vacation? Rainforests are a popular destination for those interested in eco-friendly adventures.

Costa Rica is a spectacular vacation destination for those who want to view unspoiled nature in a breathtaking setting. Most of its rainforests are on the southern Pacific Coast and the Caribbean lowlands and include Manuel Antonio National Park, Corcovado National Park, Puerto Viejo de Sarapiqui, and Braulio Carillo National Park. Tourists love the eco-friendly tourism, the wide variety of options to view the rainforest – whether it's via a guided canopy tour, zip line, a trek through the rainforest, aerial tram, or a night tour there's something for everyone. Through the lush jungle, visitors can see many species of birds, lizards, and mammals such as the sloth, howler monkeys, capuchin monkeys and squirrel monkeys. In addition to guided tours, visitors can also go bird watching, whale watching, have a dolphin encounter, white water raft, sail or kayak, scuba, tour a coffee plantation or just relax on the beach.

Costa Rica is also home to many magnificent waterfalls. Guided tours are available and can be done by foot, on horseback, or consider a rafting/waterfall rappelling combo tour. La Fortuna waterfall combines all the idyllic wildlife and unspoiled rainforest and a breathtaking view of the waterfall. The Celeste Waterfall in Tenorio Volcano National Park glows blue a few times a year, making this a spectacular visit. El Chorro and Nauyaca Waterfalls, both on the Pacific coast, are two more spectacular sites. Finally, Savegre Waterfall near Los Quetzales National Park takes about an hour to reach but the nearly 100 feet tall waterfall is well worth it.

Thinking about waterfall vacations, Angel Falls in Canaima National Park, Venezuela is a trip many waterfall enthusiasts will find breathtaking. At 3,211 feet high, this is the highest waterfall in the world. Fed by rainfall from tropical clouds, the falls precipice is known as the Mountain of the God of Evil and Devil's Mountain. Visitors travel by motorized canoe down the Carrao River to the lagoon where they can then get out and hike through the jungle to view the spectacular falls – it's a trek, but a the dramatic views of this magnificent waterfall are unforgettable.

Another waterfall-oriented destination is Africa's Victoria Falls. Located between Zimbabwe and Zambia, it's twice as tall as Niagara Falls and known as "Smoke and Thunder." Visitors can schedule a flight tour of the falls to get panoramic up-close views, or choose micro light or helicopter rides. In addition to visiting the falls, tourists can swim below the falls, schedule lion walks, walk with cheetahs and take elephant back trails. There are also several other falls in the vicinity, which makes this an adventure to remember.

With its lush rainforests and many waterfalls, a trip to Hawaii could be the destination you've dreamed of. If you choose to visit Hanakapi'ai Falls in Kauai, Hawaii you'll take an invigorating trek through lush bamboo forests, volcanic-rock cliffs and view this breathtaking 300-foot waterfall in the middle of a rainforest but still close to the beach. Not too far away is Opaekaa Falls. Though not accessible through hike or river, the falls are gorgeous. An easy to moderate hike through the rainforest can take you to Mount Waialeale, a shield volcano and the second highest point on Kauai.

Although these are just a few suggestions, there are lush tropical rainforests and spectacular waterfalls all over the world and can make for a rejuvenating and relaxing respite for the whole family.

CHAPTER 4

INTERESTING VOLCANIC VACATIONS

The red glow glimmers across the lush jungle. There's a rumble across the rainforest as smoke begins to waft over the glowing peaks of the distant volcano. Soon hot lava begins to spill. If the exotic call of a volcanic vacation beckons, here are some suggestions of places to visit.

While Hawaii is home to numerous volcanoes – Mauna Loa and Mauna Kea, both in Hawaii and in Maui, Hawaii's Kilauea is one of the more popular destinations. Though smaller than the nearby Mauna Loa, Kilauea is the most famous and most active volcano in the Hawaiian Islands, and has been erupting continually since 1983. Legend holds that it is the home of Pelehonuamea, the Hawaiian goddess of fire. Visitors often elect to stay at Volcano House, a hotel located within Hawaii

Volcanoes National Park. The hotel overlooks Halema'uma'u Crater at the summit of Kilauea and its restaurant, The Rim, offers not only delicious locally grown food but also spectacular views of the volcano in all its glory – a definite must-see.

Another popular volcanic destination is Costa Rica's Mt. Arenal. The view of this volcano feels like something out of an adventure tale –lush jungle, a body of water, and then a perfectly formed mountain peak, complete with smoke wafting from the tip. The volcano was the most active volcano in Costa Rica until 2010, when the volcano entered an indefinite resting phase. However, visitors still enjoy visits to this beautiful site where they can also hike through the rainforest at Arenal National Park, zip line through the jungle, white water raft through rivers and explore nearby waterfalls.

Mt. St. Helens in Washington State is a popular volcanic destination within the continental U.S. Visitors can stop by the Mount St. Helens Visitor Center at Silver Lake, a restaurant and helicopter tours are available at the Hoffstadt Bluffs Visitor Center.

The Johnston Ridge Observatory has good views of the north face of the volcano. Nearby Ape Cave Washington is a 2.5

mile cave created by an eruption of Mt. St. Helens over 2000 years ago.

Italy's Mt. Vesuvius, which destroyed the cities of Pompeii and Herculaneum in 79 CE, is another volcanic site worth a visit. Although Mt. Vesuvius hasn't erupted since 1944, it still occasionally emits steams of lava. The nearby ruins of Pompeii are an extraordinary place to visit – at once soberingly sad but also amazing in archaeological finds. In addition, Stromboli, off the north coast of Sicily, isn't too far away from Mt. Vesuvius. One of Italy's three active volcanoes, Stromboli has been continually erupting for 2000 years. Guided tours lead tourists climbing up the volcano where they can look into the crater for spectacular views or take a nighttime boat tour to see the glowing lava at night.

Finally Krafla, in Iceland, is another popular volcanic destination. Experience incredible views as you trek through fields of black lava and geothermal pits. Tourists describe it like being on another planet. Iceland is also a place one can view the Northern Lights, an added bonus from Mother Nature.

When planning a volcanic vacation, consider that while the volcanoes available for tourism are open because experts believe they are safe, volcanoes can and do occasionally erupt without warning. Safety experts recommend that tourists keep on the trails, follow the rules – some sites only allow guided tours or viewing from specific locations – to ensure that your vacation is memorable for all the right reasons.

CHAPTER 5

CONSIDER CAVE EXPLORATION
FOR YOUR NEXT VACATION

Yearning to try something new and adventurous on your next vacation? Have no fears of enclosed spaces? Cave exploration, or spelunking, may be the vacation for you. Here are some destinations and tips for a cave vacation to remember.

Kentucky's Mammoth Cave is one of the first caving destinations many Americans consider. One of the oldest tourist attractions in America and the most extensive cave system on earth, this sprawling 400 miles of caves is located in central Kentucky at Mammoth Cave National Park. Visitors can choose to stay in the on-site Mammoth Cave Hotel, camp in the park, or stay at one of the many nearby off-site hotels. Multiple cave tours are available for everyone from the ultimate adventurer to the elderly. Some tours offer more accessibility than others, and sign language interpreters are available on some guided tours – the park staff recommends calling ahead for availability. Horseback riding, hiking and fishing are some of the many above-ground options available at Mammoth Cave National Park.

Carlsbad Caverns, about 20 miles South West of Carlsbad, New Mexico contains 118 known caves underneath the Guadalupe Mountains. Cave tours vary in difficulty – some tours, like Hall of the White Giant, are strenuous and require long distance crawls and moving through tight crevices, but others, like the must-see site known as the Big Room, are accessible to visitors in wheelchairs. The nearest hotel is at the entrance of the park in White's City, but visitors who wish to camp may obtain a free permit from the park Visitor Center. In addition to the cave exploration, the park offers opportunities to see its bats fly each night at dusk from May-October.

In Mexico, the Yucatan peninsula's Riviera Maya between Playa del Carmen and Tulum contains 100 underwater caves. There are also cenotes, natural sinkholes that the Mayans believed were the entrance to the underworld. Needless to say, this vacation wonderland is very popular with cave divers.

Because there are so many caves, experienced cave divers in Mexico recommend hiring a professional guide or staying in a resort that offers guided tours for cave divers. The reward is some of the clearest water in the world, incredible visibility and perhaps a visit to the underworld.

Cueva de Cristales, or Cave of Crystals, is another spectacular cave to visit in Mexico. Discovered in 2000 by miners and located below the Naica Mountain in the Chihuahuan Desert of Mexico, the Cueva de Cristales contains some of the largest natural crystals ever found.

Near Saltzburg, Austria the Eisriesenwelt Ice Caves in Werfen are home to 30 miles of ice caves – some of the largest in the world. Hour and a half long tours are available. Be prepared for a long trek to get there – and guides recommend bringing a hat and mittens, but the views are breathtaking.

Finally, the Son Doong Cave in , is the largest known cave passage in the world. Discovered in 1991, scientists are still busy exploring this giant cave. The largest section of the cave discovered so far is 650 feet wide, 500 feet high and about 5 miles long – so large it could hold an entire city street full of skyscrapers or park a 747. The first tourist group went through the cave in August 2013, but more are sure to be on the way.

A cave adventure can take you anywhere in the world. Whether you're in an ice cave, exploring underwater sinkholes, or finding the alleged entrance to the underworld, you're definitely discovering a new world one way or the other. Enjoy!

CHAPTER 6

HOW TO CREATE A NORTHERN
LIGHTS VACATION

The Northern Lights are nature's seasonal light show visible in the north between late fall and spring. Caused by an interaction of charged particles with the earth's magnetic field, these lights are best visible in the north latitudes between fall and spring. Here are some ideas for creating a Northern Lights vacation to remember.

The lights are most visible in the far north – specifically between latitudes 65 and 72. Some of the best destinations for viewing include Norway, Finland, Sweden, Denmark, Iceland, Greenland, Scotland, Russia, northern Canada and Alaska.

If you don't want to leave the United States, Alaska may be your destination of choice. Experts say that Alaska's location makes it almost guaranteed that you'll see the lights. They recommend choosing a remote location far from city lights – the outskirts of Anchorage, Fairbanks, Denali and the Yukon Territory as good sites for stunning views.

Other English-oriented destinations include northern Canada – specifically the provinces of Ontario, Calgary, Yukon Territory and Manitoba. Some companies offer RV rentals to tour areas where the lights are visible. Scotland is another Northern Lights destination, but their weather often makes viewing prohibitive. January is considered the best month for viewing in Scotland, particularly in the Isle of Skye, Orkney Isles, Aberdeen, the Northern Highlands and Dunnet Head.

Scandinavia is another prime location for viewing Northern Lights. Travel options in Norway, Finland and Sweden include Northern Lights cruises, excursions that include dog sledding, snowmobile safaris, and reindeer and moose safaris. Sweden's Abisko National Park is considered one of the best places in the world to view the Northern Lights and they offer an in-park hotel that has a chair lift up to the top of the mountain where views are spectacular.

Anywhere outside a city in Iceland or Greenland can be an excellent choice for dramatic panoramic views of the Northern

Lights. Iceland also has numerous waterfalls and volcanoes to visit for further adventure. Russia is a bit more location-specific – the best locations are Murmansk, Siberia, and the Kola Peninsula. The same is true for Denmark – one must travel far north to the remote Faroe Islands, where it's rainy 200 days out of the year. Experienced travellers recommend a two-week stay in the Faroe Islands for the best chances of seeing the lights.

There are also Northern Lights cruises – destinations include Alaska, Norway and the UK. The bonus of a cruise is that rather than having a base in town and making late-night treks into the dark and chilly wilderness, the cruise can take you to a remote location that also happens to be a few minutes walk from your cozy bed. Many cruise ships offer wake-up calls to alert you of the Northern Lights. Aboard a cruise you'll also have plenty of alternate activities for those times when the conditions aren't ripe for viewing the lights.

Whatever your destination, a trip to view the Northern Lights could be the trip of a lifetime. You may want to keep in mind that if you happen to arrive during a snowstorm or a cloudy streak, you may have to extend your stay in order to see the lights. Some suggest planning your trip to avoid a full moon as its light could interfere with viewing. In planning your trip, you might want to consider what other tourist activities there may be in the area just in case you find yourself in subprime viewing conditions. If you travel in season, bring warm clothes and a sense of adventure for stunning views of one of nature's marvels.

CHAPTER 7

CREATIVE WAYS TO TRAVEL WITH CHILDREN

Are we there yet? We've all been there – either as the bored child waiting endlessly as the car travels through the Badlands of South Dakota, or as the frustrated parent trying to keep the peace as the kids duke it out in the back seat. What are some creative ways to make this family trip one they'll remember forever?

Some parents create a "gift bag" idea. Half way through the trip, each child receives a mystery gift bag with activity books, coloring materials, Colorforms to stick on the window or travel inside. Other parents set aside lots of small gifts and dole them out every hour or two, saving the best ones for the more difficult points in the trip. Items could include fruit roll ups, bubble gum, pipe cleaners, Mad Libs, maze puzzles, window markers, or – for those especially long trips, a box set that coveted TV show your child loves to watch.

Consider packing a small notebook and pencils or markers for each child to play some old time games on the way. There's always the Alphabet Game, I-Spy, the license plate game, Scavenger Hunts, counting cows, the initials game, and paper and pencil games such as MASH, Tic Tac Toe, the dot and line game, cootie catchers/fortune tellers.

Want to make the trip educational? Some parents test their children's memories and reinforce where they've travelled and what they did by playing a family trip trivia game each night. Each correct answer can score a piece of candy or the winner gets to choose which bed in the hotel, etc. Questions like, "Where did we wake up yesterday?" "What was the name of the mountain range we saw?" "Which major river did we pass?" "Which U.S. President was born in this state…" are all great ways to remember the trip and learn something.

Maps – whether they're old-school giant, foldable maps or an app from your smart phone – can be a great way to teach your children some geography and also answer the age-old "are we there yet" question. You can map the route you plan to take and have your child let you know how far away it is until the next stop, chart out interesting things to view along the way, or compare whether it's better to take route A or route B to get to Grandma's.

Other ideas: have kids make paper bag puppets – decorate the bags using markers or art supplies and then create a puppet show.

Singing in the car is a classic way to spend a road trip – think of the old camp songs you used to sing as a kid. Or what about 80s songs that your kids don't know? Karaoke versions of all kinds of songs are available for download or streaming for your trip.

Books on tape can be a great way to pass the time. Everything from Harry Potter and Charlie and the Chocolate Factory to the Hobbit can be a great way to bond. Some families enjoy listening to comedy albums from family-oriented comedians like Bill Cosby or Ellen DeGeneres.

Finally, with the entire family trapped in a small box with no clear escape, now's a great time to talk. This is a great time to tell old funny stories about your grandma and grandpa, that funny thing your uncle did when he was a kid, how Mom and Dad met. Soak up that time together and make the time memorable. That's what a family vacation is all about.

CHAPTER 8

CREATIVE WAYS TO TRAVEL
WITH A DISABILITY

Traveling is never easy. Traveling with a disability requires extra planning. Here are some ideas to make your next trip smooth sailing.

Consider booking as much as possible in advance so that you leave fewer things up to chance. Let the airline know in advance that you will be traveling with a disability. TSA has a help line and a website dedicated to travelers with disabilities and medical conditions and they address everything from diabetic travelers to travelers who have difficulty waiting in lines or have difficulty being touched. Experienced travelers recommend that travelers with disabilities arrive about an hour earlier than suggested, know your rights and be assertive – many travelers recommend bringing airline policies with you to just in case you need to reinforce your rights, such as the ability to bring a guide dog or liquid medications. Just as many travelers will mark their bag with a bright ribbon for easy identification you might want to mark your wheelchair, cane or crutches so that they're not mixed up with the airline's equipment. Travelers recommend keeping your own chair with you as long as possible to avoid mix-ups.

When selecting a hotel, be sure the receptionist knows that you need an accessible room and be sure they know which accommodations you need. Visual fire alarms or visual door knock indicators? Is there a braille room service menu? You may want to ask if the bathrooms in particular are accessible. Does the room have a roll-in shower for travelers using wheelchairs? What about a transfer seat? You may want to make sure the elevators are large enough for a wheel chair, if necessary, especially in Europe.

Although it's certainly a good ideas to have all necessary medications and supplies with you – in the original bottle with prescription information – many pharmacies will let you temporarily transfer a prescription from one pharmacy to another. This means that if you forgot something, you can call your home pharmacy and they can likely transfer the prescription to a nearby pharmacy. Also, if you're concerned about traveling with medications that require refrigeration you could simply transfer the prescription to pick up at your destination.

Remember that your hotel's concierge can help book you tours with various accommodations such as a taxi with a wheelchair lift or museum tours with audio/visual aids. However, the truth is once you're sightseeing you have less control – this is where creativity is key. Some travelers bring a different wheel chair (lighter with pop-off tires) and bungee cords in case the chair won't fit in the trunk. Some travelers that don't normally require a wheel chair might benefit from renting one while on vacation. You can also rent accessible cars or hire a driver to take you in an accessible car. Many times public transportation has a special lift or a carriage ride through the park that is accessible – calling ahead can help get details ahead of time and book a reservation. Is there an audio tour available? What about braille guides? Also, sometimes when an older tourist attraction doesn't have a public elevator there might be a freight elevator – it's worth asking.

You may want to keep in mind that what one country deems accessible might be totally different than what another country considers accessible. Sometimes you'll find a creative solution to an accessibility issue and other times you'll make new friends who have solutions. If you plan ahead, keep an open mind and keep your sense of adventure you're sure to have a great trip.

CHAPTER 9

TIPS FOR TAKING CREATIVE VACATION PHOTOS

Ah, vacation. Get away from it all. Sleep in. Read magazines, visit new places... and within a day or two you're ready for a challenge. For those of you who always want to accomplish something, even on vacation, here are some tips for creating the most creative vacation photos.

First, consider what you can do to stress the unusual. If you take the same picture in front of the Grand Canyon that everyone else in the world does, where's the creativity? Can you try it from a new angle? Consider what the picture would look like from up high or down low. What about through a doorway? Focusing on something specific such as intricate carvings or a beautiful window can make a big difference. Another idea is to try snapping that classic monument at an unusual time of day. What does the Eiffel Tower look like at dawn or dusk?

You probably have lots of pictures of your kids on the beach. Consider focusing on the details: your five-year-old's hands as she packs the sand on her sand castle, or holding the crab she found? How are those flip-flop tans coming along? Rather than focusing on the fireworks themselves, what about look of wonder on your child's face as he watches them?

Candid shots are a great way to capture what really was going on during your vacation. Sometimes the unusual backgrounds are the best pictures - one favorite family photo shows two girls reading books in beach chairs with two giant port-a-potties in the background. It's a picture no one else had and made everyone smile.

Once you've done some candid shots, consider going in the opposite direction with fun poses. Yes, that photo in front of the with your husband trying in vain to straighten the Leaning Tower of Pisa can be a cliché, but if this is who you are, have fun with it. Watching the sunset on a beach? That sunset will fit right into the top of your almost-empty ice cream cone and will make a cool picture to remember. Kids playing on the beach during the sunset? You can position them so that the setting sun becomes a ball, and so on. Are there a lot of statues in the town you're visiting? Some people have posed with them to create clever pictures that turn the statue into a flirt, an anachronism using your iPhone or anything else you can dream up.

Playing with distance and perspective, you can create some fun camera illusions. Some ideas: make a helicopter and an ant look about the same size on your drink, take a photo that looks as if you're reaching up to squeeze a cloud, or that skyscraper. Maybe a giant holding a beach pail is about to cover your two "frightened" children... let your imagination run wild.

Finally, there are lots of technical ways to get some really creative vacation photos. The Canon series of cameras has several creative filter settings – the miniature effect, for example, makes a life-sized landscape look like a miniature model train set. Explore the settings on your camera or apps available if you're shooting on your phone. There are hundreds of possibilities for taking panoramic shots, making your photos look old fashioned or 70s style, whitening teeth – the possibilities are endless.

One of the best ways to ensure creative photos from varied perspectives? Make sure everyone on the trip has a camera, and consider giving out a prize for the most creative shot. You'll have unique pictures and a vacation to remember.

Printed by Libri Plureos GmbH in Hamburg,
Germany

9 786069 837139